WELCOME TO THE U.S.A.
KENTUCKY

Written by Ann Heinrichs   Illustrated by Matt Kania
Content Adviser: Bill Bright, Historian

The Child's World

Published in the United States of America by The Child's World®
PO Box 326 • Chanhassen, MN 55317-0326
800-599-READ • www.childsworld.com

Photo Credits

Cover: David Muench/Corbis; frontispiece: Kevin R. Morris/Corbis.

Interior: Corbis: 30 (Kevin R. Morris), 33 (Bettmann); Getty Images: 14 (Photographer's Choice/Michael Townsend), 18 (Hulton|Archive/American Stock); Chris Jones/Kentucky Cola Mining Museum: 26; Kentucky Department of Parks: 13; Kentucky Folk Art Center: 22; Kentuckytourism.com: 6, 25, 29; Knox County Chamber of Commerce: 9; Land Between The Lakes: 10; Library of Congress: 8; Allison McCowan/The (London) Sentinel-Echo: 18; Kirk Schlea/Danville-Boyle County Convention and Visitors Bureau: 34; Shaker Village of Pleasant Hill, KY: 17.

Acknowledgments

The Child's World®: Mary Berendes, Publishing Director

Editorial Directions, Inc.: E. Russell Primm, Editorial Director; Katie Marsico, Associate Editor; Judith Shiffer, Assistant Editor; Matt Messbarger, Editorial Assistant; Susan Hindman, Copy Editor; Melissa McDaniel, Proofreader; Peter Garnham, Matt Messbarger, Olivia Nellums, Chris Simms, Molly Symmonds, Katherine Trickle, Carl Stephen Wender, Fact Checkers; Tim Griffin/IndexServ, Indexer; Cian Loughlin O'Day, Photo Researcher and Editor

The Design Lab: Kathleen Petelinsek, Design and art production

Library of Congress Cataloging-in-Publication Data
Heinrichs, Ann.
    Kentucky / by Ann Heinrichs.
        p. cm. — (Welcome to the U.S.A.)
    Includes index.
    ISBN 1-59296-375-7 (library bound : alk. paper) 1. Kentucky—Juvenile literature.
I. Title. II. Series.
    F451.3.H45 2006
    976.9—dc22   2004026165

Ann Heinrichs is the author of more than 100 books for children and young adults. She has also enjoyed successful careers as a children's book editor and an advertising copywriter. Ann grew up in Fort Smith, Arkansas, and lives in Chicago, Illinois.

About the Author
Ann Heinrichs

Matt Kania loves maps and, as a kid, dreamed of making them. In school he studied geography and cartography, and today he makes maps for a living. Matt's favorite thing about drawing maps is learning about the places they represent. Many of the maps he has created can be found in books, magazines, videos, Web sites, and public places.

About the Map Illustrator
Matt Kania

On the cover: Kentucky's Cumberland Gap is covered in mist.
On page one: Does this colt look like a future champion to you?

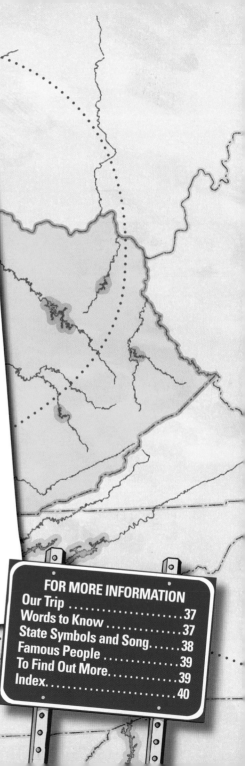

OUR KENTUCKY TRIP

4

WELCOME TO
KENTUCKY

Ready for a tour of the Bluegrass State? That's Kentucky! Just follow the car on that dotted line. Or else skip around. Either way, you'll have lots of fun. You'll learn some amazing things, too.

You'll explore caves and coal mines. You'll cheer your favorite racehorse. You'll enjoy a taste of **pioneer** life. And you'll even get to know Daniel Boone.

Are you ready? Then buckle up, and let's hit the road!

As you travel through Kentucky, watch for all the interesting facts along the way.

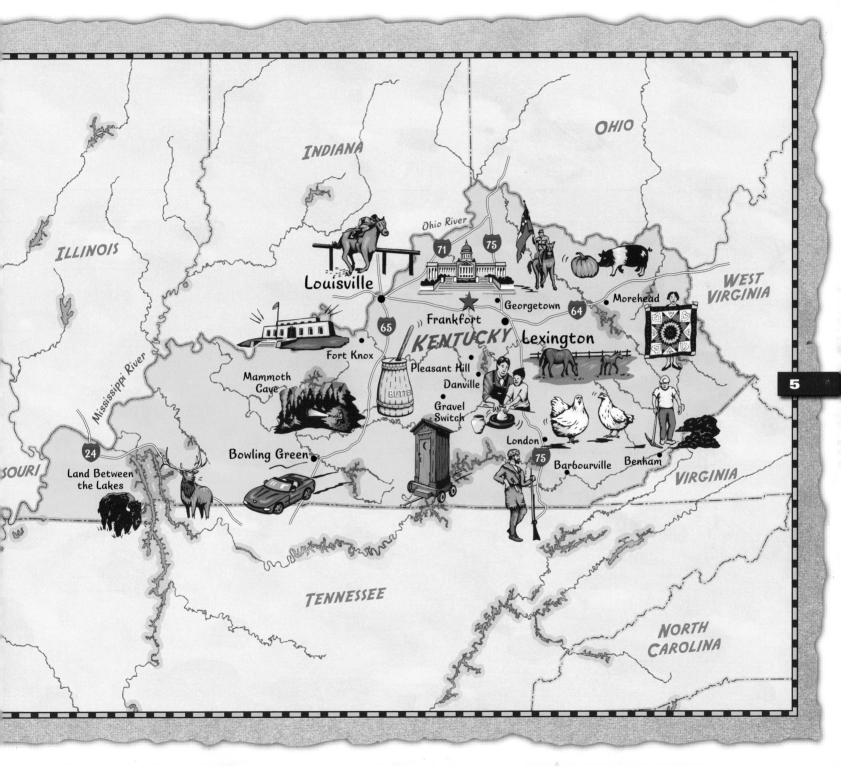

INDIANA

OHIO

ILLINOIS

WEST VIRGINIA

Ohio River

Louisville

71 75

Frankfort

KENTUCKY

Georgetown

64 Morehead

Lexington

Fort Knox

65

Mammoth Cave

BUTTER

Pleasant Hill

Danville

Gravel Switch

London

75 Barbourville Benham

Bowling Green

Land Between the Lakes

24

Mississippi River

SOURI

VIRGINIA

TENNESSEE

NORTH CAROLINA

Ready for a workout? Tour Mammoth Cave!
It's the longest cave in the world.

6

Tighten up your **hard hat.** Strap on those knee pads, too. You're taking the Wild Cave Tour in Mammoth Cave!

Mammoth Cave is Kentucky's most famous natural site. It's in the Pennyroyal Region in southwestern Kentucky. The Bluegrass Region is in north-central Kentucky. Lots of horses and cattle graze there.

Many mountains rise in eastern Kentucky. They're part of the Appalachian mountain range.

Big rivers create some of Kentucky's borders. The Ohio River outlines its entire northern border. The Mississippi River forms the western border.

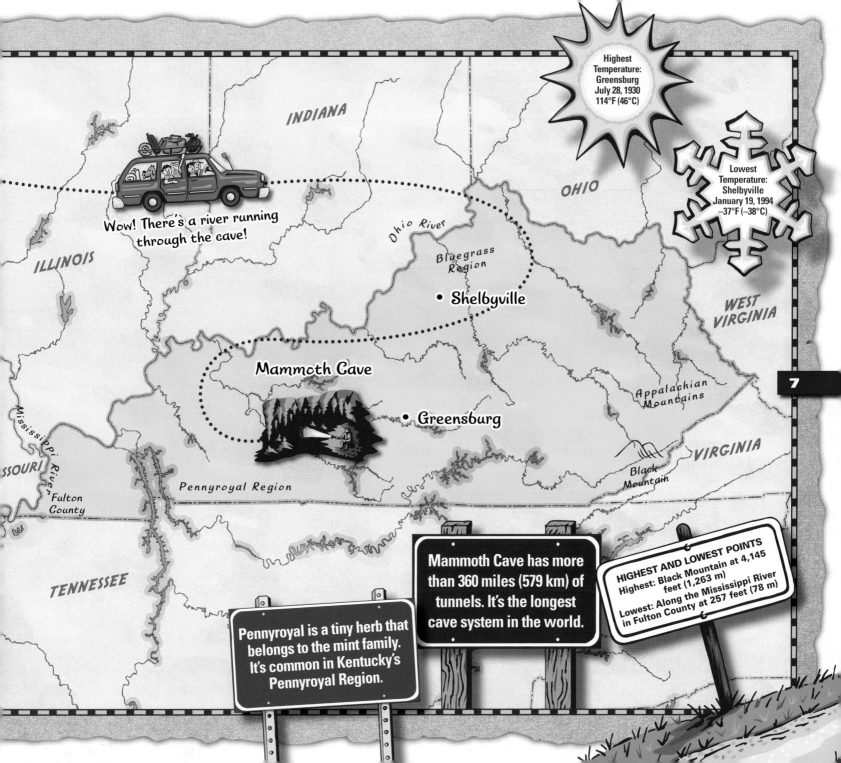

INDIANA

OHIO

ILLINOIS

WEST VIRGINIA

Ohio River

Bluegrass Region

Highest Temperature: Greensburg July 28, 1930 114°F (46°C)

Lowest Temperature: Shelbyville January 19, 1994 −37°F (−38°C)

Wow! There's a river running through the cave!

• Shelbyville

Mammoth Cave

• Greensburg

Appalachian Mountains

Mississippi River

Fulton County

Pennyroyal Region

Black Mountain

VIRGINIA

SSOURI

TENNESSEE

Pennyroyal is a tiny herb that belongs to the mint family. It's common in Kentucky's Pennyroyal Region.

Mammoth Cave has more than 360 miles (579 km) of tunnels. It's the longest cave system in the world.

HIGHEST AND LOWEST POINTS
Highest: Black Mountain at 4,145 feet (1,263 m)
Lowest: Along the Mississippi River in Fulton County at 257 feet (78 m)

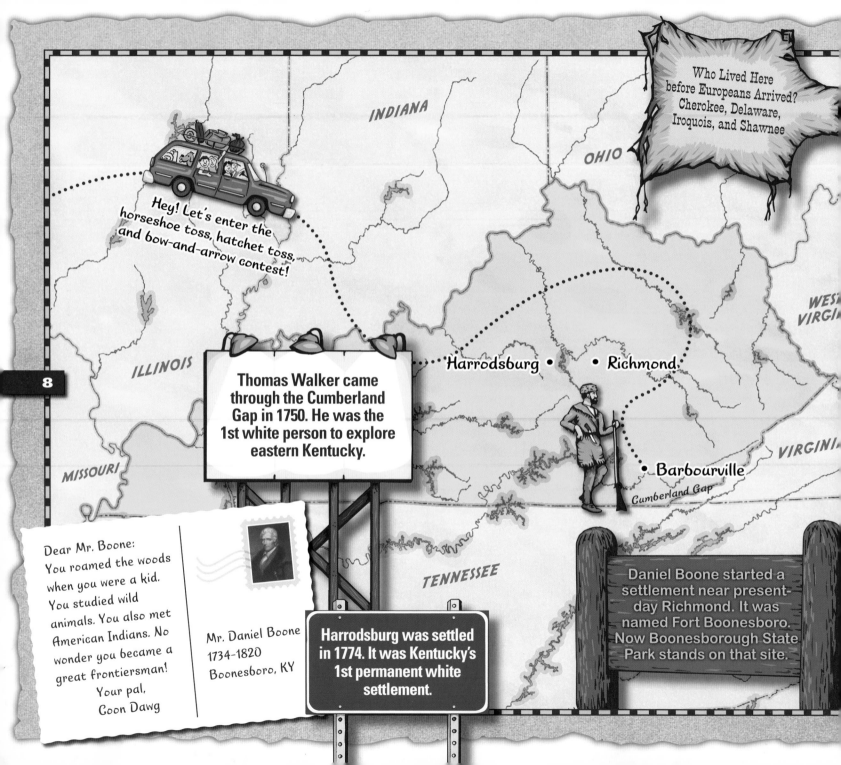

Who Lived Here before Europeans Arrived? Cherokee, Delaware, Iroquois, and Shawnee

INDIANA

OHIO

WEST VIRGINIA

Hey! Let's enter the horseshoe toss, hatchet toss, and bow-and-arrow contest!

ILLINOIS

Harrodsburg •   • Richmond

Thomas Walker came through the Cumberland Gap in 1750. He was the 1st white person to explore eastern Kentucky.

MISSOURI

• Barbourville

Cumberland Gap

VIRGINIA

Dear Mr. Boone:
You roamed the woods when you were a kid. You studied wild animals. You also met American Indians. No wonder you became a great frontiersman!
Your pal,
Coon Dawg

Mr. Daniel Boone
1734-1820
Boonesboro, KY

Harrodsburg was settled in 1774. It was Kentucky's 1st permanent white settlement.

TENNESSEE

Daniel Boone started a settlement near present-day Richmond. It was named Fort Boonesboro. Now Boonesborough State Park stands on that site.

The Daniel Boone Festival in Barbourville

Put on your **breeches** and hunting shirt. It's the Daniel Boone Festival in Barbourville!

This festival celebrates **frontiersman** Daniel Boone. He explored the Cumberland Gap Region. He wanted to cut a wide trail there. Then pioneers could move west of the Appalachians.

Boone helped build the Wilderness Road in 1775. He knew the road cut through Cherokee land. He met with the Cherokee. They agreed Boone could have land for the road. Soon thousands of pioneers poured into Kentucky. Boone guided many of them.

Would you make a good frontiersperson? Visit Barbourville and find out!

The Wilderness Road was once a trail used by buffalo and American Indians. For 50 years, it was the main road to Kentucky and Tennessee.

10

Huge bison, or buffalo, munch on the grass. Enormous elk wander nearby. This was a common sight 200 years ago. But you can still see it today. You're visiting the Elk and Bison Prairie. It's at Land Between the Lakes in southwestern Kentucky.

This area was once rich with wildlife. But hunters wiped out the elk and bison. The herds were built up again in this park.

Kentucky still has lots of wildlife. Forests cover almost half the state. Deer, bobcats, and foxes live there. So do mice, moles, and squirrels. Eagles and hawks soar overhead.

Bison peacefully munch on prairie grass.

Land Between the Lakes has a herd of fallow deer. These small deer are originally from Europe and Asia. They run with a stiff-legged bounce.

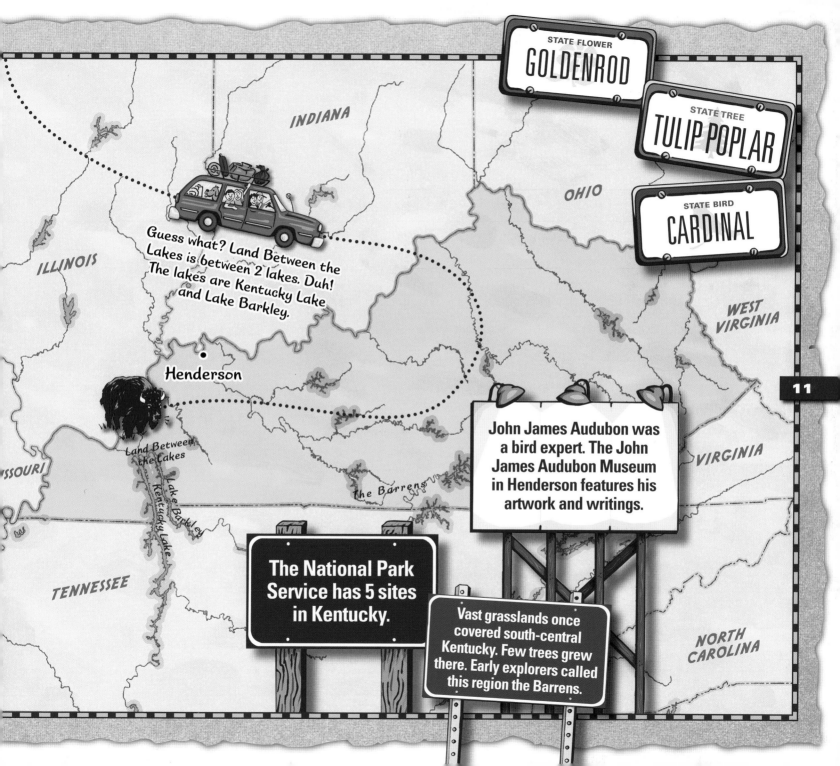

STATE FLOWER
GOLDENROD

STATE TREE
TULIP POPLAR

STATE BIRD
CARDINAL

INDIANA

OHIO

ILLINOIS

WEST VIRGINIA

Guess what? Land Between the Lakes is between 2 lakes. Duh! The lakes are Kentucky Lake and Lake Barkley.

Henderson

Land Between the Lakes

Lake Barkley

Kentucky Lake

the Barrens

MISSOURI

VIRGINIA

John James Audubon was a bird expert. The John James Audubon Museum in Henderson features his artwork and writings.

The National Park Service has 5 sites in Kentucky.

TENNESSEE

Vast grasslands once covered south-central Kentucky. Few trees grew there. Early explorers called this region the Barrens.

NORTH CAROLINA

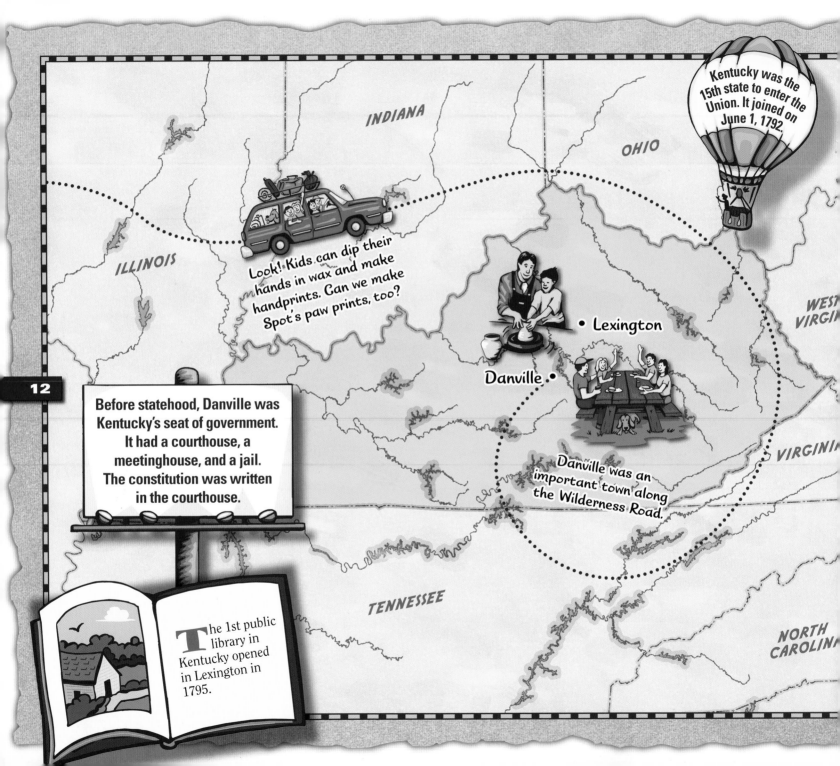

INDIANA

OHIO

Kentucky was the 15th state to enter the Union. It joined on June 1, 1792.

ILLINOIS

WEST VIRGINIA

Look! Kids can dip their hands in wax and make handprints. Can we make Spot's paw prints, too?

• Lexington

Danville •

VIRGINIA

Before statehood, Danville was Kentucky's seat of government. It had a courthouse, a meetinghouse, and a jail. The constitution was written in the courthouse.

Danville was an important town along the Wilderness Road.

TENNESSEE

NORTH CAROLINA

The 1st public library in Kentucky opened in Lexington in 1795.

Make some pottery. Get your face painted. Or take a horse-and-buggy ride. Where is all this going on? At the Historic **Constitution** Square Festival in Danville!

Constitution Square is a famous spot in Kentucky. That's where Kentucky adopted its first constitution. A constitution was required for becoming a state.

But wait—let's back up in time. Great Britain had thirteen **colonies** in North America. Present-day Kentucky was part of the Virginia colony. The colonies fought Britain in the Revolutionary War (1775–1783). They won their freedom. Then they became the United States of America. Kentucky separated from Virginia and became a state.

Want to learn how to make a flint? Just stop by Danville for a lesson!

13

Wow! Look at those columns along the hall. Each one weighs more than an elephant!

14

Kentucky's state capitol is very fancy. It's almost like a palace! The center of the building rises seven stories high. There are huge stairways and grand halls. But the builders didn't forget Kentucky's pioneer days. Paintings of Daniel Boone decorate the third floor.

This building houses Kentucky's state government offices. The state government has three branches. One branch is the General Assembly. It makes the state's laws. The governor leads another branch. It carries out the laws. Judges make up the third branch. They decide if someone has broken a law.

Does a king live here? No, this fancy building is the capitol in Frankfort.

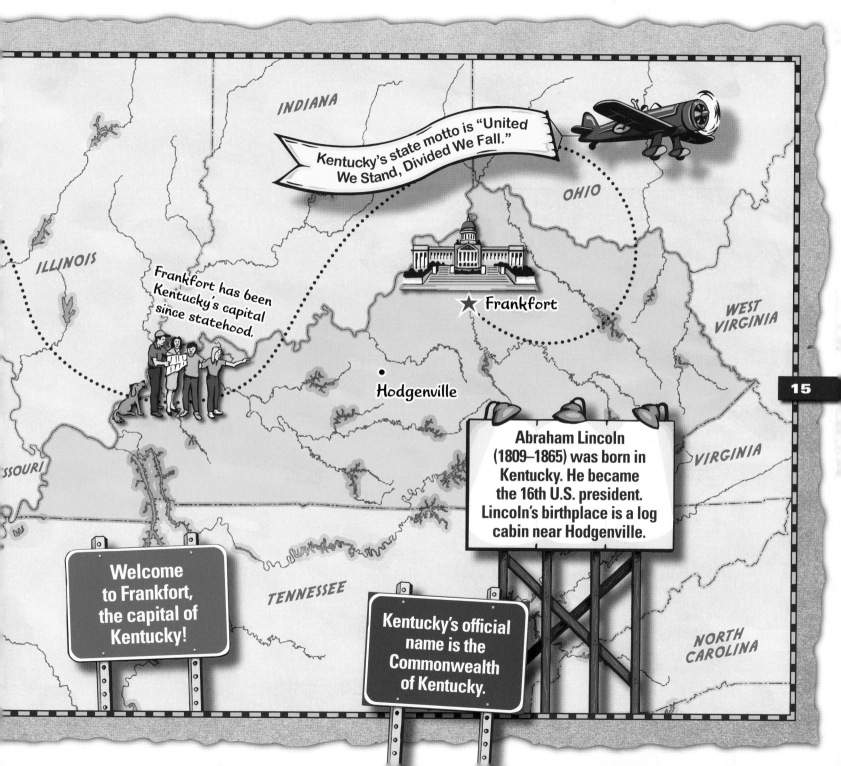

INDIANA

Kentucky's state motto is "United We Stand, Divided We Fall."

OHIO

ILLINOIS

Frankfort has been Kentucky's capital since statehood.

★ Frankfort

WEST VIRGINIA

MISSOURI

Hodgenville

Abraham Lincoln (1809–1865) was born in Kentucky. He became the 16th U.S. president. Lincoln's birthplace is a log cabin near Hodgenville.

VIRGINIA

TENNESSEE

Welcome to Frankfort, the capital of Kentucky!

Kentucky's official name is the Commonwealth of Kentucky.

NORTH CAROLINA

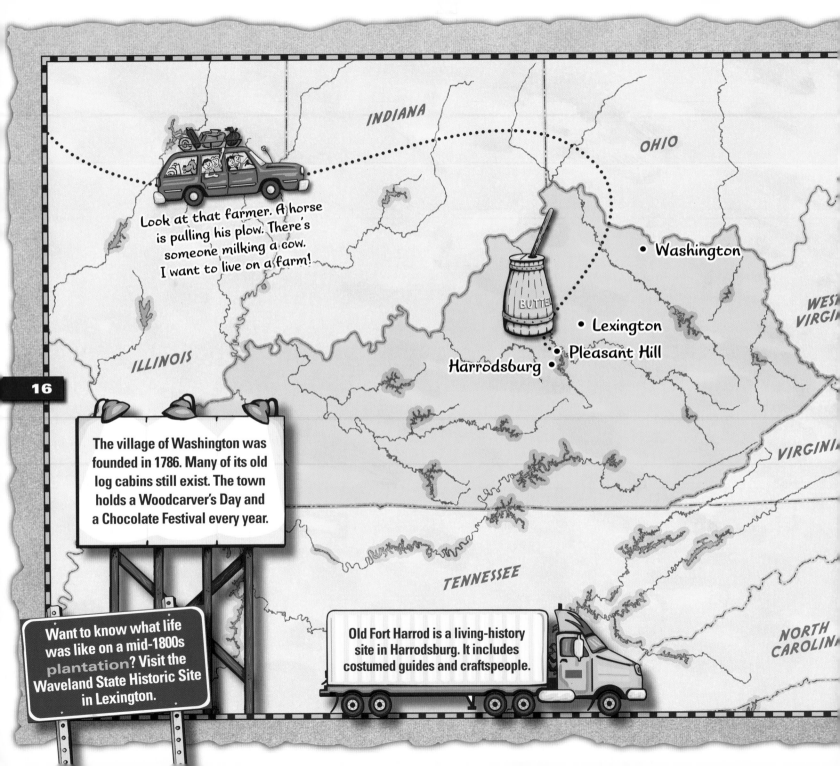

INDIANA

OHIO

• Washington

WEST
VIRGINIA

Look at that farmer. A horse
is pulling his plow. There's
someone milking a cow.
I want to live on a farm!

BUTTER

• Lexington
• Pleasant Hill

Harrodsburg •

ILLINOIS

The village of Washington was
founded in 1786. Many of its old
log cabins still exist. The town
holds a Woodcarver's Day and
a Chocolate Festival every year.

VIRGINIA

TENNESSEE

NORTH
CAROLINA

Want to know what life
was like on a mid-1800s
plantation? Visit the
Waveland State Historic Site
in Lexington.

Old Fort Harrod is a living-history
site in Harrodsburg. It includes
costumed guides and craftspeople.

Shaker Village of Pleasant Hill

Walk from one cottage to another. Here's a broom maker. There's a woodworker. Someone else is making butter. You feel like you've stepped back in time!

You're strolling through Shaker Village of Pleasant Hill. Craftspeople are hard at work there. They show how Pleasant Hill villagers once lived.

The Shakers were a religious group. They settled at Pleasant Hill in the early 1800s. The Shakers were hardworking. They raised crops, fruit trees, and cattle. They made sturdy household goods by hand. High-quality Shaker crafts became famous.

The Shakers changed how brooms were made. This style of broom is from the 1820s.

John Morgan raided several Kentucky towns.
He wanted the South to win the Civil War.

Kentucky's Tobacco Wars took place from 1904 to 1909. Small-scale farmers burned the barns and fields of people who sold tobacco to bigger companies.

Morgan's Raid in Georgetown

Bang! Pow! Kaboom! Watch out—it's Morgan's Raid!

People in Georgetown act out this battle every year. It took place during the Civil War (1861–1865). The war was between Northern and Southern states. The North, or Union side, was against slavery. Southern states were for it. They formed the Confederacy.

Kentucky didn't want to take sides. It ended up staying in the Union. John Hunt Morgan was a Confederate general. He led several raids in Kentucky. He destroyed Union supplies and caused lots of trouble. Finally, the Union won the war.

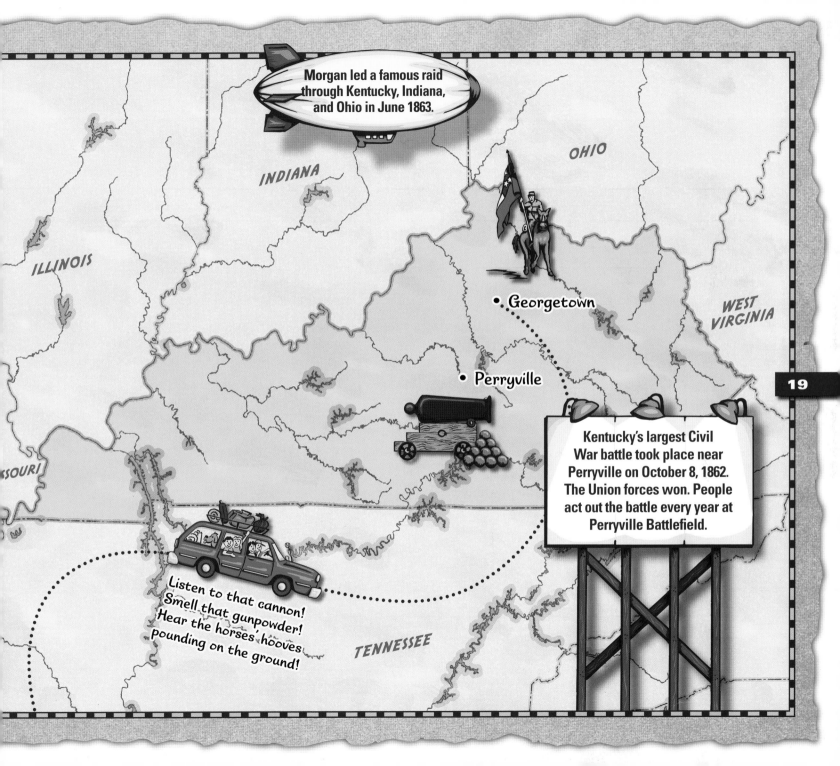

Morgan led a famous raid through Kentucky, Indiana, and Ohio in June 1863.

OHIO

INDIANA

ILLINOIS

WEST VIRGINIA

• Georgetown

• Perryville

Kentucky's largest Civil War battle took place near Perryville on October 8, 1862. The Union forces won. People act out the battle every year at Perryville Battlefield.

MISSOURI

Listen to that cannon! Smell that gunpowder! Hear the horses' hooves pounding on the ground!

TENNESSEE

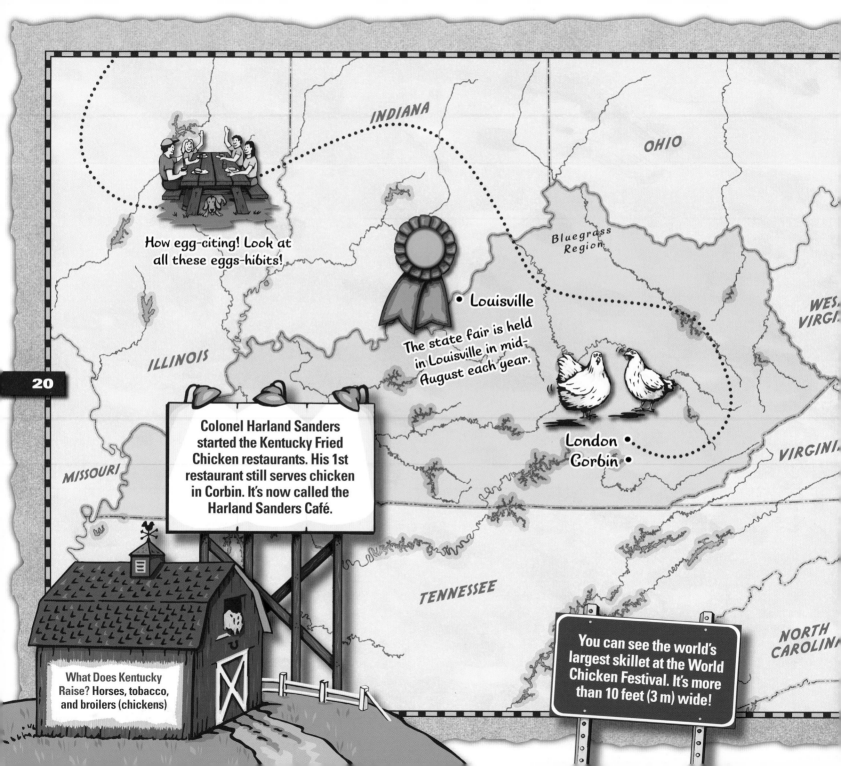

How egg-citing! Look at all these eggs-hibits!

INDIANA

OHIO

Bluegrass Region

• Louisville

The state fair is held in Louisville in mid-August each year.

WES. VIRGI.

ILLINOIS

London •
Corbin •

VIRGINIA

Colonel Harland Sanders started the Kentucky Fried Chicken restaurants. His 1st restaurant still serves chicken in Corbin. It's now called the Harland Sanders Café.

MISSOURI

TENNESSEE

NORTH CAROLINA

What Does Kentucky Raise? Horses, tobacco, and broilers (chickens)

You can see the world's largest skillet at the World Chicken Festival. It's more than 10 feet (3 m) wide!

The World Chicken Festival in London

The World Chicken Festival includes a contest for crowing, strutting, and clucking!

First, there's an egg hunt. Then there's an egg-in-a-spoon race. Next? The egg toss and the chicken scratch. You're taking part in the Chick-O-Lympics! It's part of London's World Chicken Festival.

Chickens are important farm products in Kentucky. So is tobacco. It's Kentucky's leading crop.

Horses are even more important, though. Horse pastures stretch out over the Bluegrass Region. Kentucky horse farms raise thousands of horses. Many horse owners plan to race their animals. Kentucky produces some of the world's fastest racehorses!

Kids compete in a contest at London's World Chicken Festival.

21

The Kentucky Folk Art Center in Morehead

A young Kentuckian created this painting. You can view it at the Kentucky Folk Art Center.

You catch a glimpse of long-necked blue roosters. You even see the famous Wild Booger! Don't worry—they're just pieces of art. You're touring the Kentucky **Folk Art** Center. It features unusual art from the Appalachian Region.

Kentuckians enjoy many local arts and crafts. Many people make quilts and pottery. They follow patterns handed down over many years. Bluegrass music had its start in Kentucky. Country music and folk songs are popular, too.

Most residents used to live in the country. Now most Kentuckians live in cities or towns. But they still honor their country roots.

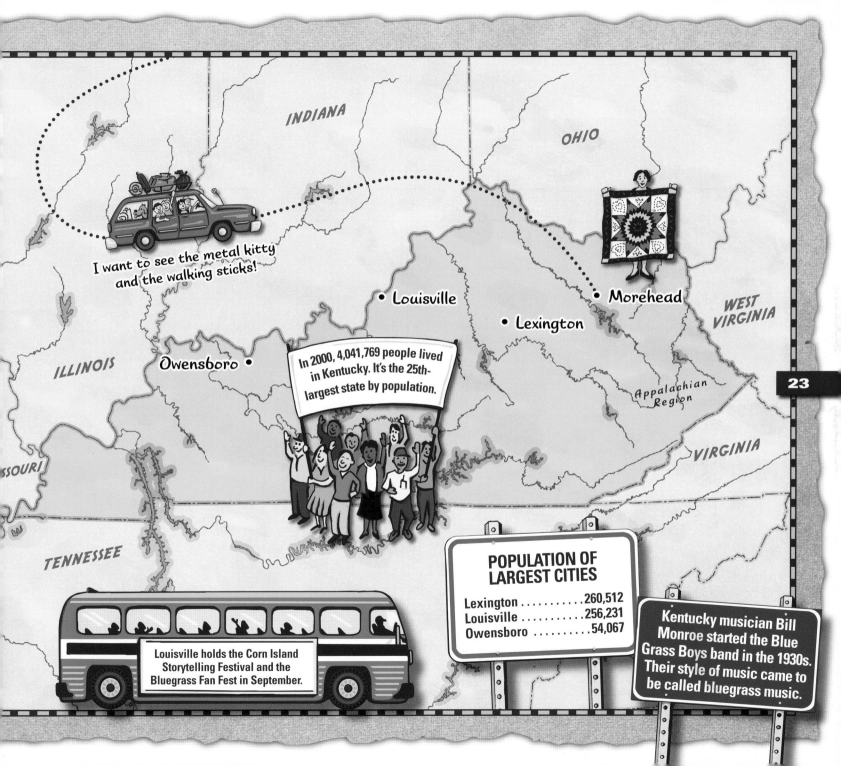

I want to see the metal kitty and the walking sticks!

• Louisville

• Lexington

• Morehead

Owensboro •

In 2000, 4,041,769 people lived in Kentucky. It's the 25th-largest state by population.

INDIANA

OHIO

WEST VIRGINIA

ILLINOIS

Appalachian Region

VIRGINIA

SSOURI

TENNESSEE

23

POPULATION OF LARGEST CITIES

Lexington 260,512
Louisville 256,231
Owensboro 54,067

Louisville holds the Corn Island Storytelling Festival and the Bluegrass Fan Fest in September.

Kentucky musician Bill Monroe started the Blue Grass Boys band in the 1930s. Their style of music came to be called bluegrass music.

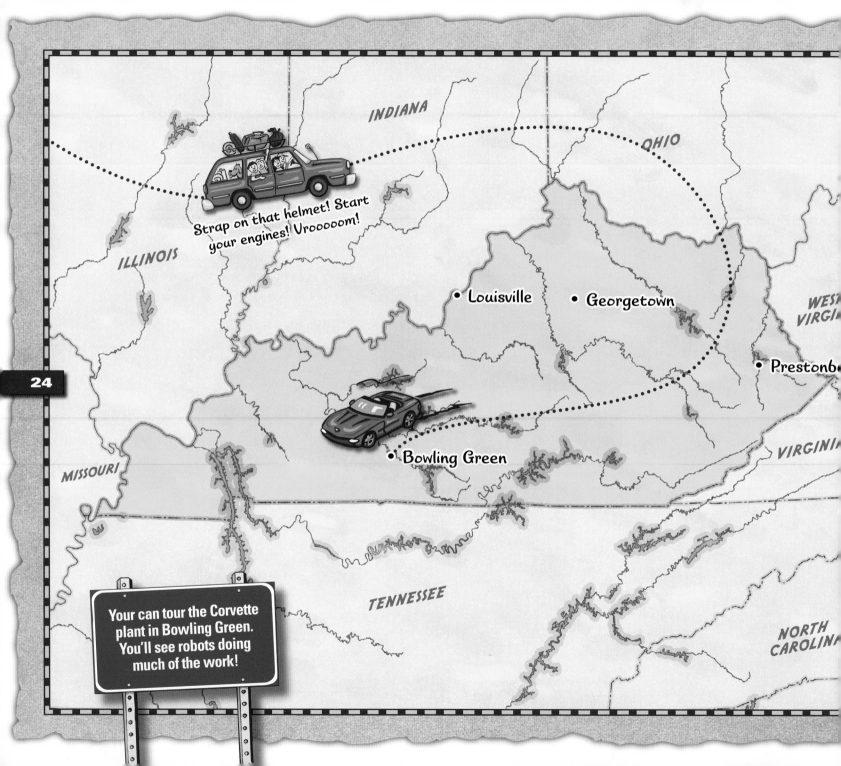

INDIANA

OHIO

Strap on that helmet! Start your engines! Vrooooom!

ILLINOIS

• Louisville

• Georgetown

WEST VIRGINIA

• Prestonb

MISSOURI

• Bowling Green

VIRGINIA

TENNESSEE

NORTH CAROLINA

Your can tour the Corvette plant in Bowling Green. You'll see robots doing much of the work!

The Mini-Corvette Challenge in Bowling Green

Are you crazy about Corvettes? These sporty little cars are really sharp! Just check out the Mini-Corvette Challenge. It's a go-cart race. But the go-carts have Corvette bodies! The race is in Bowling Green. That's where Corvettes are made.

Kentucky relied on farming for a long time. Tobacco and horses brought in lots of income. Miners dug tons of coal from Kentucky's mines, too.

Farming and mining slowed down by the 1950s. Manufacturing was growing fast, though. Many car factories opened in Kentucky. Now cars are made in Georgetown and Louisville. And don't forget Bowling Green and its Corvettes!

Are you a fan of sports cars? The Corvette has been around since 1953.

The East Kentucky Science Center is in Prestonburg.

Benham's Kentucky Coal Mining Museum

Want to learn about coal mines? Put on your hard hat and head to Benham!

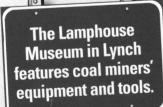

The Lamphouse Museum in Lynch features coal miners' equipment and tools.

The winding path is dark and spooky. You feel like you're deep underground. You're touring a model of a coal mine. It's in Benham's Kentucky Coal Mining Museum.

Kentucky is a top coal-mining state. It has two main coal-mining regions. One is in the far northwest. The other is in the eastern Appalachian Region.

Kentucky has lots of big factories, too. Cars and trucks are the major factory products. Many factories make car and truck parts. Other factories make medicine, paint, and machinery.

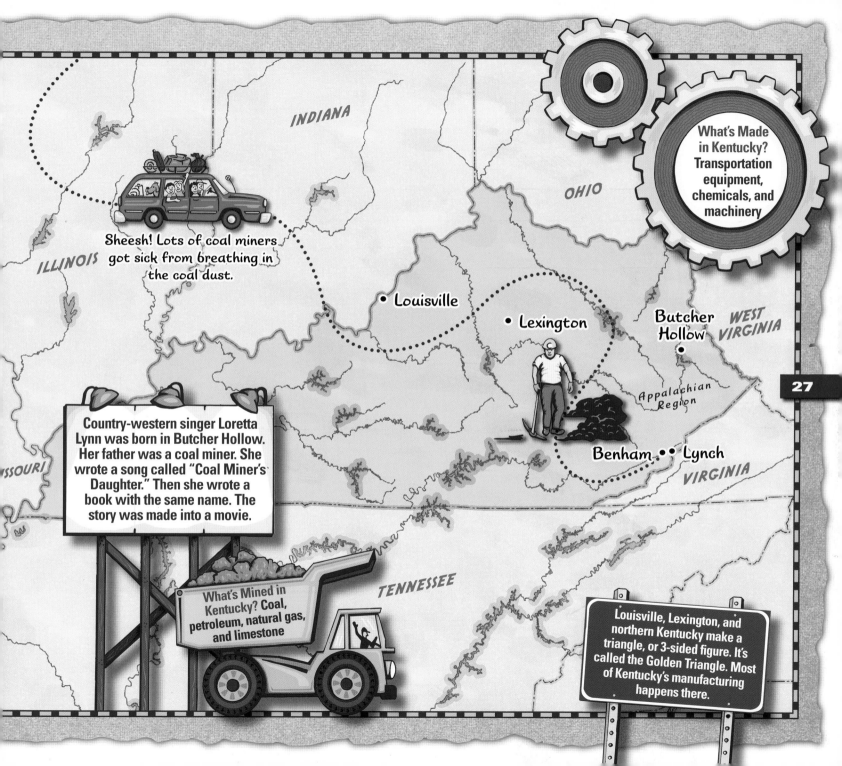

INDIANA

OHIO

ILLINOIS

Sheesh! Lots of coal miners got sick from breathing in the coal dust.

• Louisville

• Lexington

Butcher Hollow •

WEST VIRGINIA

Appalachian Region

What's Made in Kentucky? Transportation equipment, chemicals, and machinery

Country-western singer Loretta Lynn was born in Butcher Hollow. Her father was a coal miner. She wrote a song called "Coal Miner's Daughter." Then she wrote a book with the same name. The story was made into a movie.

MISSOURI

Benham •• Lynch

VIRGINIA

What's Mined in Kentucky? Coal, petroleum, natural gas, and limestone

TENNESSEE

Louisville, Lexington, and northern Kentucky make a triangle, or 3-sided figure. It's called the Golden Triangle. Most of Kentucky's manufacturing happens there.

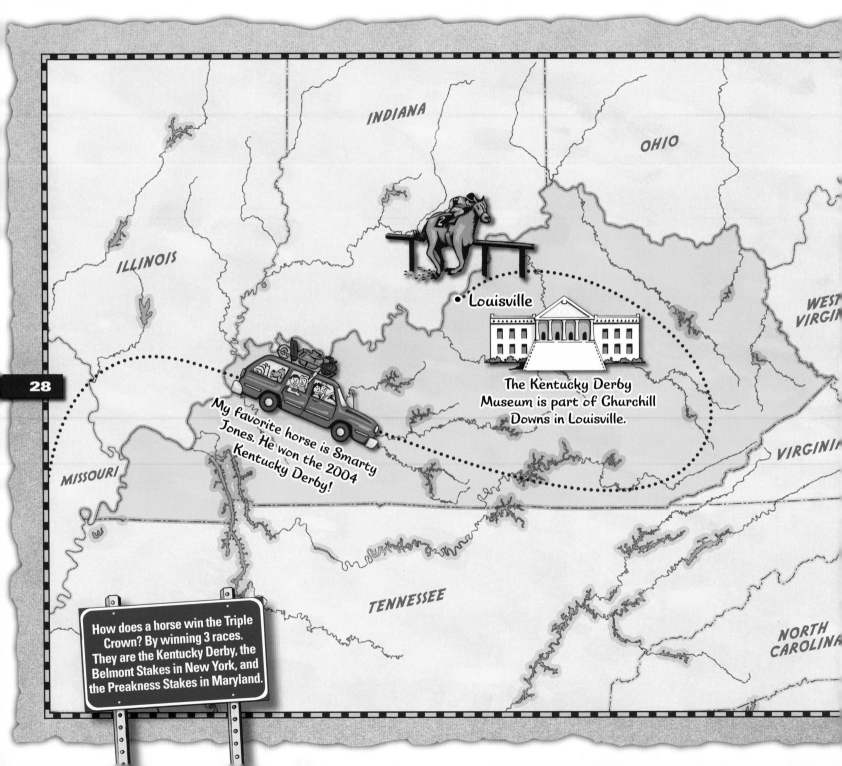

INDIANA

OHIO

ILLINOIS

WEST VIRGINIA

• Louisville

The Kentucky Derby Museum is part of Churchill Downs in Louisville.

My favorite horse is Smarty Jones. He won the 2004 Kentucky Derby!

MISSOURI

VIRGINIA

TENNESSEE

NORTH CAROLINA

How does a horse win the Triple Crown? By winning 3 races. They are the Kentucky Derby, the Belmont Stakes in New York, and the Preakness Stakes in Maryland.

The Kentucky Derby at Churchill Downs

Churchill Downs was built in 1875.

And they're off! The horses dash out of the gate. 'Round the track they go. Your favorite is pulling ahead!

You're at the country's most exciting horse race. It's the Kentucky Derby at Churchill Downs. This race is Kentucky's biggest sports event. It happens on the first Saturday in May. People come from around the world to watch.

Many Kentuckians enjoy baseball. They cross the northern border into Ohio. There they can watch Cincinnati Reds games.

Kentuckians also love the great outdoors. Some go fishing, boating, or camping. Others explore caves or hike through the mountains. As you see, there's plenty to do in Kentucky!

Do you like horses? Be sure to visit Lexington.

White fences surround acres of pasture. Beautiful horses trot around or just graze. This is Lexington's Kentucky Horse Park. It's in the heart of Kentucky's Bluegrass Region.

You'll see almost fifty breeds of horses at the park. There's a daily horse show in the summer. Many breeds perform there.

One barn is a home for draft horses. These are horses that pull heavy loads. You can tour the park in a horse-drawn carriage. It's pulled by draft horses. A blacksmith works at the park, too. He pounds out iron to make horseshoes.

Kentucky Horse Park has many museums and exhibits. If you love horses, it's the place for you!

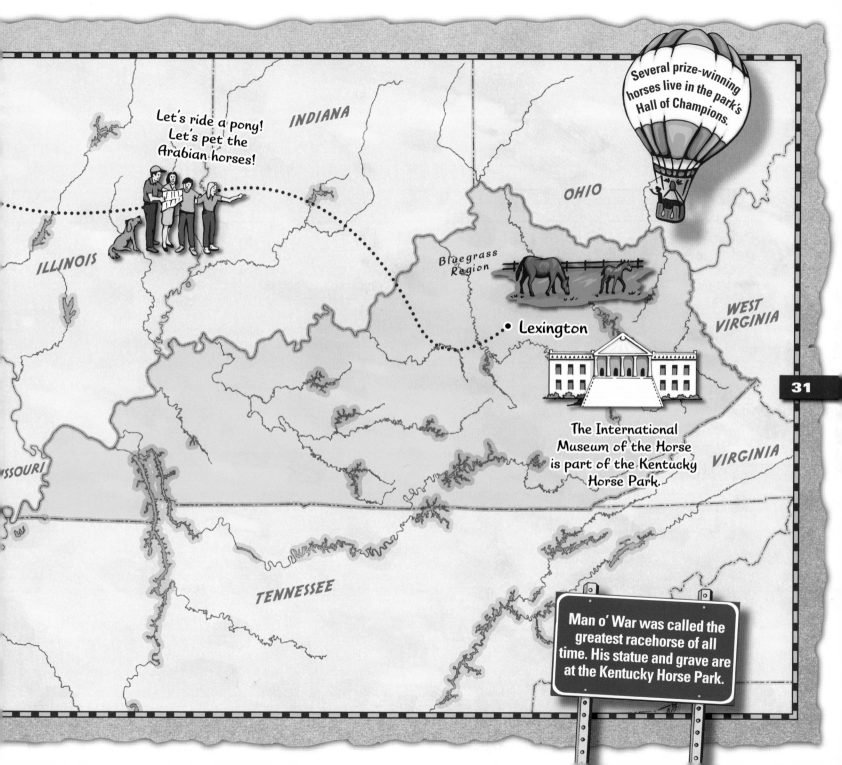

Let's ride a pony! Let's pet the Arabian horses!

INDIANA

ILLINOIS

OHIO

Several prize-winning horses live in the park's Hall of Champions.

Bluegrass Region

WEST VIRGINIA

• Lexington

MISSOURI

The International Museum of the Horse is part of the Kentucky Horse Park.

VIRGINIA

TENNESSEE

Man o' War was called the greatest racehorse of all time. His statue and grave are at the Kentucky Horse Park.

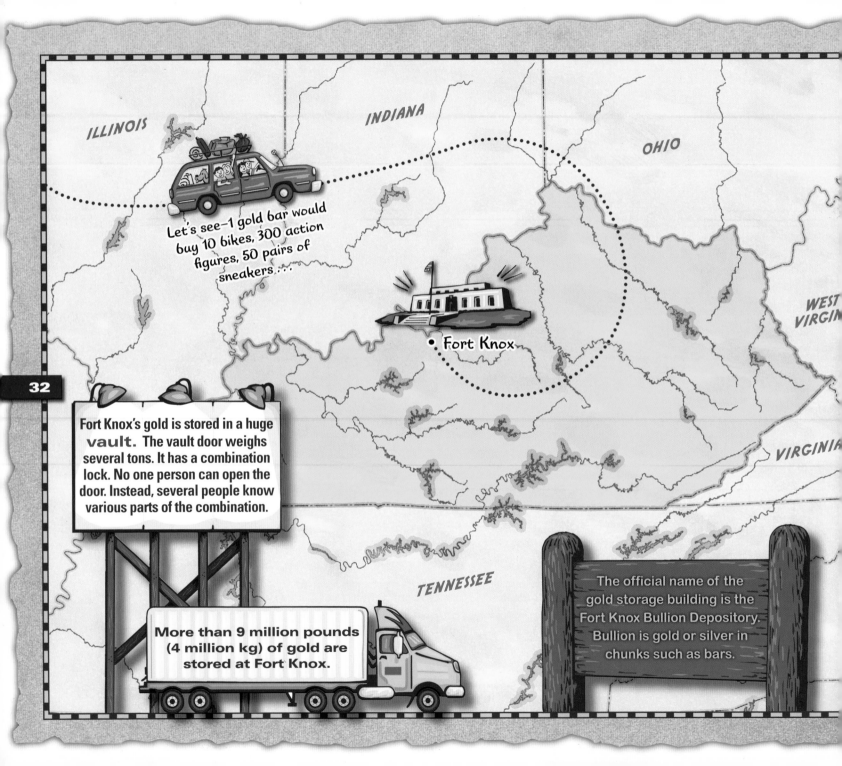

ILLINOIS

INDIANA

OHIO

WEST VIRGINIA

Let's see—1 gold bar would buy 10 bikes, 300 action figures, 50 pairs of sneakers....

• Fort Knox

Fort Knox's gold is stored in a huge **vault.** The vault door weighs several tons. It has a combination lock. No one person can open the door. Instead, several people know various parts of the combination.

TENNESSEE

VIRGINIA

More than 9 million pounds (4 million kg) of gold are stored at Fort Knox.

The official name of the gold storage building is the Fort Knox Bullion Depository. Bullion is gold or silver in chunks such as bars.

The U.S. Gold Depository at Fort Knox

Bars of gold are stacked to the ceiling. They're worth billions of dollars! Just one bar is worth more than $16,000!

This is the U.S. gold **depository.** It's a well-guarded building in Fort Knox. The U.S. government stores much of its gold there. You'll never get near that gold, though. No visitors are allowed. Still, it's fun to think about!

This building is very strong and safe. It was useful during World War II (1939–1945). Many important items were stored there. One was the U.S. Declaration of Independence. Others included Great Britain's crown jewels. These jewels belong to the royal family.

Fort Knox is home to billions of dollars in gold.

On your mark! Get set! Push your toilet!

The announcer yells to begin the race. "Ladies and gentlemen, start your toilets!" You're in the tiny town of Gravel Switch. And you're watching the Great Outhouse Blowout. It's an outhouse race!

An outhouse is an outdoor restroom. It's shaped like a phone booth. Outhouses were used before people had indoor plumbing.

The race has lots of rules. Each outhouse has to have a name. All outhouses must roll on wheels. A five-person team races each outhouse. Two people push it. Two people pull it. And one person rides inside.

Winning the race isn't everything. There's also an award for the most creative outhouse!

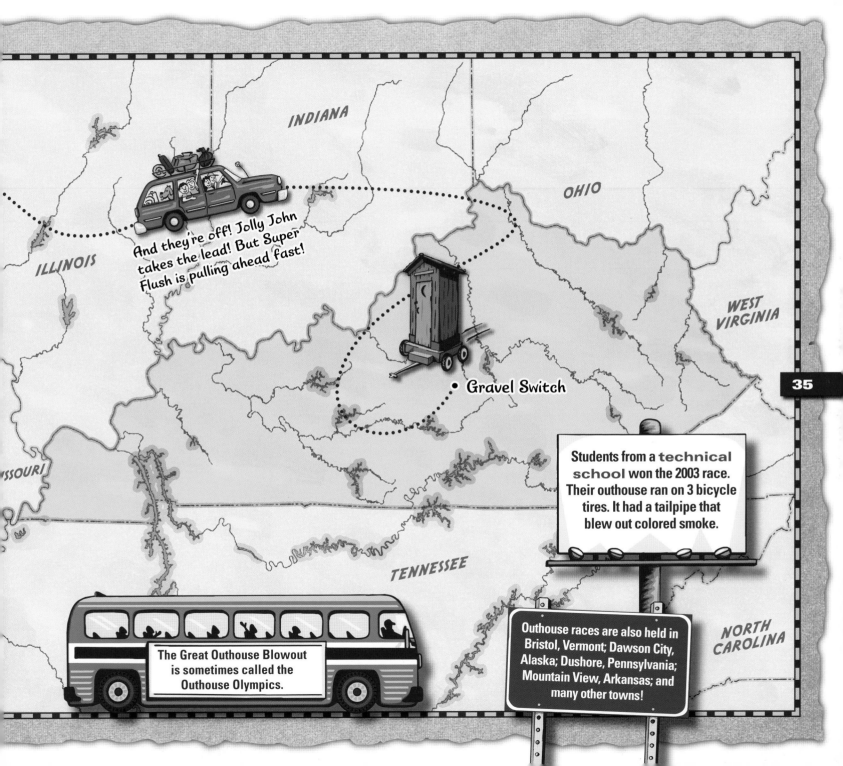

35

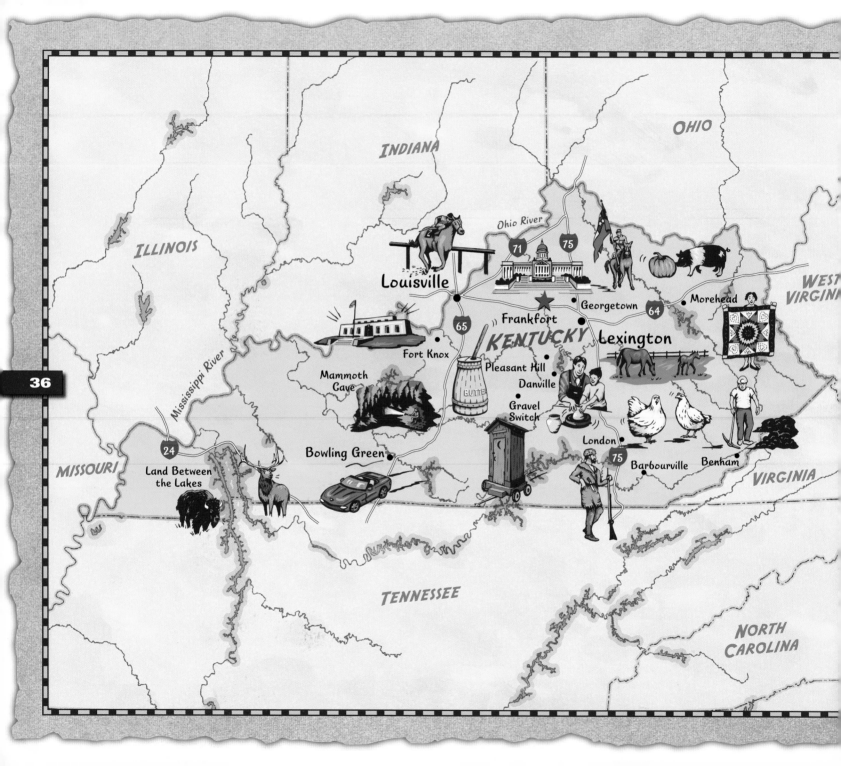

OUR TRIP

We visited many places on our trip! We also met a lot of interesting people along the way. Look at the map on the left. Use your finger to trace all the places we have been.

Where can you see a tiny flower called the Pennyroyal? See page 7 for the answer.

How does a fallow deer run? Page 10 has the answer.

Who drew pictures and wrote articles about birds? See page 11 for the answer.

How wide is the world's largest skillet? Look on page 20 for the answer.

What is Kentucky's largest city? Page 23 has the answer.

How did Smarty Jones become famous? Turn to page 28 for the answer.

What museum is a part of the Kentucky Horse Park? Look on page 31 and find out!

What is stored in Fort Knox's vault? Turn to page 32 for the answer.

WORDS TO KNOW

breeches (BRICH-iz) knee-length pants that are tight at the bottom

colonies (KOL-uh-neez) new lands with ties to a parent country

constitution (kon-stuh-TOO-shuhn) a basic set of laws for a country or state

depository (di-POZ-i-tor-ee) a place where things are stored

folk art (FOHK ART) art by people who have little or no artistic training

frontiersman (fruhn-TIHRZ-man) someone who is skilled at living and traveling in an unexplored, forested region

hard hat (HARD HAT) a hat made of hard material to protect the head

pioneer (pye-uh-NEER) someone who moves into an unsettled area

plantation (plan-TAY-shuhn) a large farm that raises mainly 1 crop

technical school (TEK-nuh-kuhl SKOOL) a school that teaches useful skills such as plumbing and car repair

vault (VAWLT) a room where money and other valuables are stored

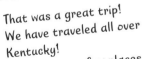

That was a great trip! We have traveled all over Kentucky!

There are a few places that we didn't have time for, though. Next time, we plan to visit the Double Stink Hog Farm in Georgetown. This famous farm used to raise pigs and other animals. But now visitors come to enjoy the sweet corn and pumpkins!

More Places to Visit in Kentucky

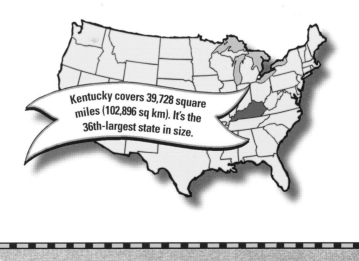

Kentucky covers 39,728 square miles (102,896 sq km). It's the 36th-largest state in size.

STATE SYMBOLS

State bird: Cardinal

State bluegrass song: "Blue Moon of Kentucky"

State butterfly: Viceroy butterfly

State fish: Kentucky spotted bass

State flower: Goldenrod

State fossil: Brachiopod

State gemstone: Freshwater pearl

State horse: Thoroughbred

State tree: Tulip poplar

State wild game animal: Gray squirrel

State flag

State seal

STATE SONG

"My Old Kentucky Home"
Words and music by Stephen Collins Foster

The Sun shines bright in my old Kentucky home,
'Tis summer, the people are gay;
The corn top's ripe and the meadow's in the bloom,
While the birds make music all the day.

The young folks roll on the little cabin floor,
All merry, all happy and bright;
By 'n by hard times comes a-knocking at the door,
Then my old Kentucky home, good night!

Chorus:
Weep no more, my lady
Oh weep no more today;
We will sing one song for my old Kentucky home,
For my old Kentucky home, far away.

FAMOUS PEOPLE

Ali, Muhammad (1942–), boxer

Boone, Daniel (1734–1820), pioneer

Breckinridge, John Cabell (1821–1875), U.S. vice president

Breckinridge, Madeline McDowell (1872–1920), women's rights activist

Clay, Henry (1777–1852), politician

Clooney, George (1961–), actor

Depp, Johnny (1963–), actor

Griffith, D. W. (1875–1948), film director

Handy, W. C. (1873–1958), blues musician

Judd, Ashley (1968–), actor

King, Pee Wee (1914–2000), country music performer

Lincoln, Abraham (1809–1865), 16th U.S. president

Lynn, Loretta (1935–), singer

Mason, Bobbi Ann (1940–), author

Monroe, Rose Will ("Rosie the Riveter") (1920–1997), American feminist hero

Powers, Georgia (1923–), Kentucky's 1st female state senator and 1st African American state senator

Sharp, Philip A. (1944–), biologist

Stevenson, Adlai (1835–1914), U.S. vice president

Thompson, Hunter S. (1939–), author

Young, Whitney M., Jr. (1921–1971), civil rights leader

TO FIND OUT MORE

At the Library

Alter, Judy. *Daniel Boone: Frontiersman.* Chanhassen, Minn.: The Child's World, 2003.

Gordon, Randy. *Muhammad Ali.* New York: Grosset & Dunlap, 2001.

Mara, Wil. *Abraham Lincoln.* New York: Children's Press, 2002.

Riehle, Mary Ann McCabe, and Wes Burgiss (illustrator). *B Is for Bluegrass: A Kentucky Alphabet.* Chelsea, Mich.: Sleeping Bear Press, 2002.

Valzania, Kimberly. *Kentucky.* New York: Children's Press, 2003.

On the Web

Visit our home page for lots of links about Kentucky: *http://www.childsworld.com/links*

Note to Parents, Teachers, and Librarians: We routinely verify our Web links to make sure they are safe, active sites—so encourage your readers to check them out!

Places to Visit or Contact

The Kentucky Department of Travel
500 Mero Street, Suite 2200
Frankfort, KY 40601
502/564-4930
For more information about traveling in Kentucky

Kentucky Historical Society
100 W. Broadway
Frankfort, KY 40601
502/564-1792
For more information about the history of Kentucky

INDEX

Bye, Bluegrass State.
We had a great time.
We'll come back soon!